Pablo Picasso

by Janet Buell

MODERN CURRICULUM PRESS

Pearson Learning Group

The word *strange* has been used by many people to describe the artwork of Pablo Picasso. Much of the art he created doesn't look like things from the world we know.

Picasso wanted to be free to create the world as he saw it. He felt a need to push against the boundaries of art and beauty. Picasso once said: "To me [beauty] is a word without sense because I do not know where its meaning comes from nor where it leads to."

You may or may not find Picasso's paintings and sculptures beautiful. He often showed people in unusual ways. He painted portraits of men and women with eyes on the sides of their heads. Sometimes he painted their noses where their eyes should be. Some of his figures have square or rectangular heads. Some look as if he cut up a picture and rearranged it.

This is a portrait Picasso made of his daughter, Maya.

Pablo Picasso was born in 1881 in Malaga, Spain. He was the first child of Maria Picasso and Jose Blasco. Picasso came from a very artistic family. His aunts and uncles were amateur artists. His father was an art teacher.

From the beginning, Picasso was an unusual child. His first spoken word was *piz*. *Piz* is short for *lápiz*, the Spanish word for pencil. He could be bad-tempered, but he also was very creative and generous. He ignored his toys and played with things he collected.

Picasso's mother didn't understand her son's bad moods and behavior. His teachers didn't understand him either. When his kindergarten teacher asked him to draw a flower, he drew a big yellow sun in a red sky. His teacher got mad. The other students just laughed.

Once Picasso painted with sauce on the walls of his family's home. Another time, he drew with charcoal on a clean bed sheet. And still another time he scratched a picture with a nail on the living room wall. His mother moved the couch in front of the drawing so his father wouldn't see it.

Picasso's mother tried to be patient with him, but it was often very difficult. She did not discuss Picasso's troublesome behavior with his father, who wanted to come home to a peaceful house.

His mother's patience finally broke one Sunday when Picasso painted directly on his sister's face. He used egg yolk as paint. He circled her eyes with bright strokes of yellow. He dabbed yolk on her cheeks. He dabbed it on the tip of her nose. He streaked her hair with the beautiful yellow color. At first, his sister thought Picasso's game was fun. Then she saw what he had done. This time, Picasso had gone too far. His mother felt she had to tell his father.

Picasso's father saw how upset his daughter and wife were. He took Picasso for a walk on the beach. There they could talk about his behavior. But Picasso could not explain why he acted the way he did. Not wanting to return home too quickly, Picasso's father lay down for a nap while his son played in the sand.

When Picasso's father awoke, he saw a beautiful line drawing of a dolphin. The dolphin arched across the wet sand. The drawing had been made with a single line. Picasso's father had never seen such a beautiful, simple drawing. He looked about for the artist, but saw only his son. When he asked his son about the drawing, Picasso explained that he had drawn the dolphin.

When they arrived home, Picasso's father asked to see the drawing behind the sofa. Picasso had scratched a picture with a nail of a man with a bow and arrow. The man rode horseback. He was hunting deer and bison that seemed to be running along the wall.

It looked like the primitive drawings of early humans. It was a wonderful sketch. Finally, his father understood. His son needed to express himself through art.

Picasso's father knew what he had to do. He had to teach his young son how to paint. He gave his son artist's canvases. He gave him paint and charcoal. He showed him how to draw. His father made Picasso draw and redraw birds and hands until they were perfect.

When Picasso was ten years old, his family moved away from sunny Malaga. They traveled to La Coruña, a dismal Spanish city where his father had gotten a new job. Picasso went to the art school where his father was professor. He learned all the techniques of art—pen and ink drawing, oil and watercolor painting, charcoal and crayon sketches. Picasso's father demanded hard work and discipline from his son. Picasso became an excellent student.

Picasso painted this self-portrait when he was fifteen years old.

In addition to teaching, Picasso's father created paintings, which he sold. The money helped pay the rent or buy food for his family. While his father was a good artist, he was not a great artist.

When Picasso was a teenager, his father began giving him some of his drawings to complete. When Picasso showed him the drawings, his father saw that his son's work was much better than his own. His father knew that Picasso had more artistic talent than he would ever have. He gave Picasso all his art materials. It made him proud to see his son's talent. It also made him very sad. He would never match his son's talent. Picasso's father decided to give up painting.

Picasso drew and painted all the time. He took to the dark, dirty streets and painted what he saw there. He painted beggars. He painted poor children, playing in the street.

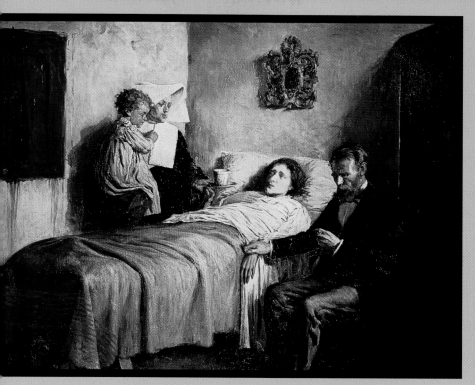

Science and Charity *was painted by Picasso when he was sixteen years old.*

Picasso painted animals too. He painted pigeons, cats, and dogs. He painted the bulls he saw at the bullfights he and his father attended.

Picasso became the art school's best student. When he was thirteen years old, Picasso had his first art show. It took place in the doorway of an umbrella maker's shop.

By the time he was fourteen, Picasso's family moved to Barcelona, Spain. Picasso applied to the art academy there. The students who went to the school were much older. To be a student at the school, an artist had to pass a painting test. Each student had a month to paint two human figures.

Picasso finished both of his works in one day. He told a friend, "I finished mine the first day . . . I studied them for a long time, and I carefully considered what I could still add to them, but I couldn't see a thing." The director of the school was impressed. He put Picasso into the advanced art classes.

By the time he was nineteen years old, Picasso had grown restless. Some of his artist friends had gone to Paris, France. At that time, Paris was the art capital of the world. Picasso's parents gave him the money to travel and experience the artistic atmosphere in Paris.

Picasso went to galleries and museums. He went to sidewalk cafes and parks. Since he hadn't yet developed a style of his own, he painted in the style of famous artists. Those artists—Monet, Renoir, Gaugin, van Gogh, Toulouse-Lautrec, and Cézanne— are still considered masters today. It was here, in Paris, that Picasso decided to take his mother's last name, Picasso, as his own.

Portrait of Jane Avril
by Pablo Picasso, 1901

Life in Paris was not easy for Picasso. He was so poor, he often went hungry. Sometimes he couldn't afford to buy paint. Other times, to keep warm, he burned his drawings in the small stove in the little room he rented.

Despite his troubles, Picasso began thinking about his artistic style. He hoped to develop an artistic style of his own. He wanted a style that would represent the way he thought about the world.

When Picasso was twenty years old, something happened that changed the way he painted. His best friend died suddenly and unexpectedly. Picasso felt alone and sad. It was now that he entered what art experts call his "Blue Period." He still painted the people he saw, but now he used mostly shades of blue. Many of the paintings he created during this time show people with faces, legs, and hands longer than they really are. Some of the figures are fixed in cramped positions.

Picasso painted The Old Guitarist in 1908, during his "Blue Period."

His painting, *The Old Guitarist*, is painted in blue. The man's head and long neck are bent over the guitar he strums with long fingers. The color blue and the cramped figure represent the sadness and loneliness Picasso felt at the time.

Many people, including his father, thought Picasso's blue paintings were very strange. But Picasso didn't worry about what other people thought. He kept painting.

This is Picasso's Family of Saltimbanques. *He painted this during his "Rose Period."*

The "Blue Period" came to an end when Picasso met a beautiful woman named Fernande in the early 1900s. Picasso and Fernande fell in love. They were very happy. Picasso's happiness could be seen in his work. He began painting in soft pinks and earth tones. The scenes he painted were happy ones. Many of the subjects in his "Rose Period" work are acrobats and circus people. The people he depicts in these paintings stand strong and proud. During this time, he began to sell his paintings and earn more money.

Picasso's mind was always searching for different and unusual ways to view the world. He wanted more than anything to find a new way of showing the weight and volume of objects on a flat canvas surface. Picasso also struggled with how to show more than one view of an object at a time. He experimented with using cubes and other geometric shapes to represent objects.

And so it was that Cubism was born. In a Cubist painting, it looks as if the artist has chopped up his subject into cubes and then rearranged them. With Cubism, Picasso felt he was finally able to capture the weight and volume of the things he painted.

Many Cubist works are hard to understand. People who saw Picasso's Cubist paintings were very critical of them. Some people were outraged by Picasso's new art form. Some critics said Cubism was an insult to what was beautiful in life and nature.

*On the left is a Cubist portrait painted by Picasso in 1910.
Can you find the figure's face? On the right is Seated Woman,
which Picasso painted in 1927 after a trip to Rome, Italy.*

There were, however, many people who liked
Picasso's new art form. They thought Cubism was a
wonderful change from tradition. The old masters
painted according to certain rules of nature, art, and
beauty. Picasso broke all those rules.

Over time, Cubism took on many looks. It became softer. It took playful turns. However, even with these changes, the subjects in Picasso's paintings still look strange to many people. The viewers aren't used to seeing eyes, mouths, and noses in different places. They aren't used to seeing the front view and side view of a violin all at once.

As much as he liked Cubism, Picasso's restless mind still searched for other ways in which to show the world. Eventually, he returned to more traditional styles of art. As always, he added his own special twist. You can see this twist in Picasso's painting called *Seated Woman*. He made the woman's hands and other features larger than usual.

Picasso's mural, Guernica, shows how he felt about the horrors of war.

Picasso lived in France for most of his adult life, but he always thought fondly of his Spanish homeland. When war broke out in Spain in 1936, Picasso supported the Republicans. His support came in the form of money. At this point in his life, Picasso was a very popular artist and he was extremely wealthy. His money helped set up feeding centers for poor and hungry children in two cities. It was also used to help hundreds of Spanish refugees.

In 1937, when planes bombed the village of Guernica, Picasso decided to create a painting to protest the bombing. Picasso's painting, *Guernica*, was named after the city that was destroyed. This black, white, and gray painting measures over eleven feet high by over twenty-five feet wide. The painting did not show the actual bombing scene. But its sad tones reflect the terrible results of war.

This painting was displayed at the Spanish Pavilion at the 1937 World Exhibition in Paris. *Guernica* made Picasso famous around the world. Many feel that this is his best work.

Besides painting, Picasso enjoyed many other art forms. During the Cubist phase of his career, Picasso began adding materials other than paint onto his pictures. He added pieces of colored paper, small pieces of wood, string, and everyday objects, such as newspapers and sheets of music.

The Cubists called these pieces of art *collages*. The word *collage* comes from a French word which means "to stick."

Picasso took this idea of a collage a little further and began creating solid still lifes using materials such as cardboard, tin, and bits of junk. Sculptures that involved changing the original material were called constructions. In these sculptures, the materials were changed in some way. They were folded, cut, glued, or painted. Sculptures that didn't change the materials were called *assemblages*. In these sculptures, the materials were just simply put together.

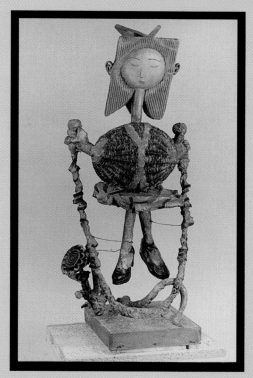

*Picasso used anything he could find
to make his playful sculptures.*

Picasso could see art in almost anything.
Sometimes he even used what people might think
of as junk to make a sculpture. One piece, called
Girl Jumping Rope, was made from junk that Picasso
found at a dump. The girl's face is made from a
box of chocolates. Her hair is cardboard. Her
body is made from a wicker basket, and her skirt is
made from newspaper.

Picasso made many wonderful ceramic pieces.

In his late sixties, Picasso got involved in another art form—ceramics. At first, he just decorated the pieces made by someone else. But eventually, he made his own ceramic pieces. As with previous art forms, Picasso did not follow rules. He experimented, making ceramic pieces that looked more like sculpture. Sometimes he cut designs into his pieces to add texture. He created about two thousand ceramic pieces during his life.

For years Picasso had enjoyed printmaking. He drew designs on copper plates or soft stones, and then used these designs to create complicated pictures. In 1959, he found a new material that could be used to create his prints. He started working with linoleum, which is a material used to cover floors. He cut designs into the linoleum and then used the linoleum block to make a print. He made more than three hundred of these linocuts in four years.

Picasso felt that his work kept him from getting old. He was still creating artwork when he was ninety years old. Picasso received numerous awards for his work.

Toward the end of his life, Picasso did most of his work at home in his large studio. He had become so famous that it became almost impossible to go anywhere without a huge crowd of people surrounding him.

Woman Seated in an Armchair
by Pablo Picasso

Picasso had courage to create the kind of art he loved. He did not stick with one style, but rather worked in many different styles. He continually looked for new ways to express himself. He ignored people's critical opinions. His courage gave other artists all over the world courage to create in their own ways. His work changed the world of art forever.